CALIFORNIA
A PICTURE MEMORY

Text
Bill Harris

Commissioning Editor
Andrew Preston

Captions
Louise Houghton

Editorial
Gill Waugh

Design
Teddy Hartshorn

Production
Ruth Arthur
David Proffit
Sally Connolly

Photography
Colour Library Books Ltd
International Stock Photo
FPG International

Director of Production
Gerald Hughes

Picture Research
Annette Lerner

Director of Publishing
David Gibbon

CLB 2505
© 1990 Colour Library Books Ltd, Godalming, Surrey, England.
All rights reserved.
Color separations by Scantrans Pte Ltd, Singapore.
This 1990 edition published by Crescent Books,
distributed by Outlet Book Company, Inc, a Random House Company,
225 Park Avenue South, New York, New York 10003.
Printed and bound in Italy.
ISBN 0 517 01746 6
8 7 6 5 4 3 2 1

CALIFORNIA
A PICTURE MEMORY

CRESCENT BOOKS
NEW YORK

Mark Twain didn't care for California.

It requires distance to give it charm, he said. In his opinion, the mountains, which he had to admit were imposing, need to be seen from far away to soften their ruggedness. The forests, monotonous as far as he was concerned, are better contemplated removed from their "reliefless and relentless smell of pitch and turpentine." The meadows didn't invite him to take his shoes off and run through them. He said that "the grass blades are unsociably wide apart with uncomley spots of barrens and betweens." As for San Francisco, he found it handsome at a fair distance, but its architecture on closer inspection turned out to be "old-fashioned … decaying, smoke grimed." He liked the climate there well enough, but complained that it almost never changed. "During eight months of the year," he wrote, "the skies are bright and cloudless, and never a drop of rain falls. But when the other four months come along, you will need to go and steal an umbrella. Because you will require it. Not just one day, but one-hundred-and-twenty days in hardly varying succession." He wasn't too pleased with Sacramento's climate, either. He couldn't help reminding his readers that "a very, very wicked soldier died there once and, of course, went straight to the hottest corner of perdition – and the next day telegraphed back for his blankets." But he admitted that he found it interesting to "gather roses, and eat strawberries and ice cream, and wear white linen clothes and pant and perspire at eight or nine o'clock in the morning … and at noon, put on your skates and go skimming over frozen Donner Lake, seven thousand feet above the valley, among snow banks fifteen feet deep, and in the shadow of grand mountain peaks that lift their frosty crags ten thousand feet above the level of the sea. There is transition for you! Where will you find another like it in the Western hemisphere?"

It astounded him, he said, "to hear tourists from 'the States' go into ecstacies over the loveliness of ever-blooming California." Then he pointed out, "But perhaps they would modify them if they knew how old Californians, with the memory full upon them of the dust-covered and questionable summer greens of California verdure, stand astonished, and filled with worshipping admiration, in the presence of of the lavish richness, the brilliant green, the infinite freshness, the spendthrift variety of form and species of foliage that make an Eastern landscape a vision of Paradise itself."

It is pleasing to report that California survived Mark Twain.

But apparently he wasn't alone in his opinion that it would never amount to much. It was one of the very first parts of the future continental United States to be discovered and explored. Only three years after DeSoto trekked along the Gulf Coast from Florida to the Mississippi River, Juan Rodriguez Cabrillo sailed up the Pacific Coast in search of the fabled Northwest Passage. A storm drove him into San Diego harbor and kept him there for a week. But he had orders to follow. He had been sent to find a water route to Asia, not new territory, and as soon as the weather cleared, he was on his way again. He sailed all the way up to Oregon, anticipating Mark Twain by observing California from a distance. But though he claimed everything he saw in the name of the Spanish king, he wasn't especially impressed. Nor were the people who read his reports. It took the Spanish another sixty years to get back to California. And they might not have bothered even then if Sir Francis Drake hadn't been poking around reclaiming the coast for the English and, to add insult to injury, using it as a base for attacking Spanish treasure ships bound for Mexico from the Philippines.

Things quietened down when Drake went back to England, and the Spanish forgot about California again until 1603, when King Philip III discovered some dusty old files among his father's papers. They contained a sworn statement from the crew of a ship that had been driven ashore by a storm off the California coast and said they had seen the fabulous Golden City of Quivira with their own eyes. Coronado had spent the last several years of his life wandering through the Rocky Mountains and across the Great Plains looking for it. But this seemed to be proof not only that the Golden City wasn't an Indian hoax, as many had grudgingly come to believe, but that it wasn't in Kansas, either. But when his explorers came back empty-handed, King Philip lost interest in California again and the Indians there were safe from civilization for another 165 years.

Europeans in general, and the Spanish in particular, were obsessed with the idea that God had sent them to the New World to preach the Gospel to the Indians. The missionaries who had been spreading the Word in Mexico and Central America for nearly 300 years had been Spanish Jesuits, but when they fell out of political favor and were sent home, the Franciscans who replaced them needed a new world to conquer. They found their opportunity in California, and in 1769, their leader, Father Junipero Serra, went north and established a mission at San Diego. Within seven years, he had built twenty-one of them extending up the coast as far as San Francisco. Each had a church, a center for civil affairs and a fort to protect it from outsiders with un-Christian ideas.

Whether God approved of what they did or not is a matter for theologians to discuss. But they added the burden of virtual slavery to their enlightenment of the savages. They forced the Indians to move away from their villages and farms and required them to live and work at the missions. Anyone caught escaping was imprisoned and anyone who resisted working for the support of the community or showed any signs of resenting the influence of Christianity was severely punished. The Indians went along with the idea, even though they were in their own land and outnumbered the Spanish who hadn't bothered to encourage their countrymen to settle the north along with them. That wouldn't happen until 1824, when Mexico declared its independence from Spain and began giving away California land to increase its own territorial influence. But even free land wasn't a good enough incentive for anyone except cattle ranchers and it wasn't until the 1830s, when the first pioneers began arriving from the Eastern United States, that anyone began thinking that California might be a nice place to settle down.

After that happened, official Mexico began to wonder if it hadn't overlooked something. When the American President Andrew Jackson offered them a half-million dollars for the place, they sneered at him. Ten years after that, President James Polk raised the ante to $40 million and when he was turned down, he responded by declaring war on Mexico. By the time it was all over, California belonged to the United States. And not a moment too soon. One year later, almost to the day, James W. Marshall discovered gold on land the Mexicans had given to John A. Sutter some years before to encourage him to settle the Central Valley.

Within three years more than 200,000 people arrived in California to get their piece of what the newspapers back East were calling the true El Dorado. In less than seven years, they pulled more than $450 million in gold from the hillsides and streams. Mr. Sutter couldn't stop prospectors from overrunning his 50,000-acre spread on the mother lode and he died penniless, as did his employee, James Marshall. But others got rich without touching so much as a flake of gold. Philip Armour became the country's biggest meat supplier providing food for hungry prospectors; John Studebaker, who later became an automotive pioneer, got his start in the carriage business selling them wheelbarrows; Levi Strauss made canvas pants for them and was on his way to making his name a household word. The gold rush itself lasted only five years before the prospectors were replaced by commercial mining interests and turned their attention to the silver strikes across the border in Nevada. But enough people stayed in California to make it a going concern even without gold, and the immigration still hasn't stopped. With 27,663,000 persons, it has the largest population of any state, topping New York by well over 9.8 million, and the entire population of Canada by some 2.3 million.

But if California is a nice place to live, it's also a terrific place to visit. Well over 91 percent of Californians live in cities, leaving millions of acres in their natural state. There are seven National Monuments and nine National Parks plus two National Recreation Areas and a National Seashore within California's borders. The state maintains 86 of its own recreation areas, and there are 17 National Forests in its 158,000 square miles.

It isn't possible to think of the National Parks of California without also thinking of John Muir, the great naturalist who made them a reality. But John Muir didn't spend his whole life thinking about California. In fact, in the mid-1850s, when he set out from Indiana for what he expected would be the great adventure of his life, he didn't even look west. He headed southeast and didn't stop walking until he reached the Florida Keys. His plan was to get to Cuba and study the mountains there before going on to South America to unravel some of the mysteries of the jungle and the Amazon River.

He was forced to stop at the Keys because he had run out of money on his long walk across the width of America. He didn't have any trouble finding a job, but the next leg of his trip was delayed by a long illness, and by the time he got to Cuba, he was too weak to do any mountain climbing. He decided to move on to South America anyway, but there was no ship headed in that direction and it was then that California came to mind. It would probably have been easier to get to South America as it turned out. First he had to go to New York to catch a ship bound for Panama. Then he hiked across to the Pacific side and waited for a boat heading north to San Francisco. ... And this was a man too weak to climb the mountains in Cuba.

He finally arrived in San Francisco in the spring of 1868, well rested and ready to go, but just a little bit feisty. John Muir was not a city person, and he hated San Francisco. Almost trembling with anxiety, he asked a stranger how to get out of town. He was directed to the ferry bound for Oakland and it was there that fate stepped in. Among his fellow passengers was an Englishman looking for adventure. They decided together that they'd find it in the Yosemite Valley, and a few days later when he saw it for the first time, John Muir knew that he had come home and that he'd never hack through the jungles of South America, explore the Amazon or look down on Havana from a mountaintop.

Three of California's National Parks are in the Sierra Nevada Mountains and one, Lassen Volcanic National Park, is near the spot where the Cascades meet the High Sierra. Until that spring day when John Muir bounded down the mile-deep Yosemite Valley with pen in hand, no one had ever thought much about the Sierras except as a place to get rich quick. The early California-bound pioneers had found them an impossible barrier on the eastern side. But once they got across to the western slopes they knew that the American dream was here for the taking in this glorious land of California.

But taking was all they did. They ruined forests, dirtied streams and lakes, dispersed wildlife. Not a single thought was given to preserving or replacing anything. And why should there be? Here was nature in unbelievable abundance as far as a man could see either into the distance or into the future. It may well be why the fates led John Muir to make a wrong turn on his way to South America.

Four years after he arrived at Yosemite, Congress created the world's first national park at Yellowstone. And John Muir was already sending magazine articles back east telling the world of the wonders he had found in California. Eventually, his articles suggesting park status for Yosemite became the basis for a bill in Congress, and after less than three months of Congressional debate, on October 1,1890, Yosemite became America's second National Park.

The Sierra Nevada is different from the Rockies, its neighbor a thousand miles to the east, and its next-door neighbor to the north, the Cascades, because it is a single mountain range. It is, in fact, the longest mountain range in the United States, extending 400 miles from north to south and an average of 60 miles from east to west. Its eastern slope is mostly made up of awesome cliffs, some as much as two miles high, rising straight up from the desert floor. On the other side, the drop is comparatively gentle in most places down to the 180-mile-wide Central Valley that stretches off in a sea of lush green toward the Coast Range and the Pacific Ocean some 180 miles to the west.

Among California's other natural treasures are the incredible redwood and sequoia trees. They've both been major tourist attractions from the day they were first discovered, and are usually lumped together as California's "big trees." The fact is, the coastal redwoods and the sequoias of the mountainsides aren't even related to each other.

That didn't matter to the early loggers who did their best to wipe both species from the face of the earth, and very nearly succeeded. It was hard work. And they worked for more than a hundred years to destroy what had taken nature thousands to create. Beginning with the Indians, who regarded the big trees as sacred, the lumber interests found opposition everywhere they turned, but they turned a deaf ear to the protests. There was money to be made, after all. They managed to destroy nearly all of the trees, and the only groves that are still standing are the few that have been granted Government protection.

Seeing the remaining groves today is as impressive for what you don't see as for what is there. No two are the same, and considering the fact that hundreds of groves don't exist any longer can almost move you to tears. The 275-ft. General Sherman tree in Sequoia National Park is often called the largest living thing on earth. The Park Service doesn't get too many arguments about the claim, but the sequoia named for President McKinley is more than 15 feet taller, and the redwoods further north are, on average, 40 or 50 feet higher. But none of them is as big around. General Sherman has a 36.4-ft waistline which, says the experts, makes the tree at least 4,000 years old.

Almost all of the big trees still standing were already big when the Christian era began, and their immediate environment hasn't changed much through the centuries. But by comparison, what has become of California is nothing short of incredible. Its farms produce just about every crop raised in any other part of the country, and quite a few that don't grow anywhere else. No other state produces as many grapes or peaches, lemons or avocados. California also produces more wine, more fresh eggs, more turkeys and more honey. In fact, California leads the country in the production of 48 different crops; it grows 40 percent of all the fruit and nuts in the United States and 25 percent of the vegetables. But what impresses Americans most about California is the production of movies and TV shows.

The movies arrived in California in 1902 and the star-struck were right behind. Real estate operators followed, and in less than two decades, Los Angeles, which had been a sleepy little mission town, covered 360 square miles. Then they discovered oil and it grew some more. It was one of the few cities in the country to keep on growing through the Great Depression of the 1930s. And in the 1940s, World War II brought new industry and more converts to the Southern California life style. The Los Angeles city limits enclose 465 square miles today, with an average of 6,380 people in each and every one of them.

And they keep coming. The population of California has more than doubled since 1950, and though they are more likely to arrive by plane these days, would-be Californians come with the same attitude Robert Louis Stevenson wrote about back in 1892 after making the trip by train. "It was like meeting one's wife," he said. "I had come home again – home from the unsightly deserts to the green and habitable corner of the earth. Every spire of pine along the hill-top, every trouty pool along that mountain river, was more like a blood relation to me. ... Not only I, but all the passengers on board, threw off their sense of dirt and heat and weariness and bawled like schoolboys, and thronged with shining eyes upon the platform and became new creatures within and without. ... This was indeed our destination; this was 'the Good Country' we had been going to so long."

Stevenson arrived in San Francisco twenty years after Mark Twain decided to go back to New York. On the day he left, he noted that his decision was prompted by homesickness and in his parting shot he admitted that California was "the friendliest land and livest, heartiest community on our continent."

Facing page: Redwood National Park.

Redwood National Park (these pages), approximately five hours drive north of San Francisco on Highway 101, covers more than a hundred thousand acres. The trees themselves (Sequoia sempervirens) often reach heights in excess of 300 feet. The shade they create, combined with the characteristic coastal fog, provides an ideally moist bed for ferns, shrubs and delicate wildflowers on the forest floor. It is a magical place of light and shade, giants and dwarves.

California dreaming – the state's coastal scenery, with its varied forms and moods, is a constant source of pleasure. When Europeans first discovered this rugged shore they assumed it to be that of a Pacific island. They named it after an island of gold, ruled by the mythical warrior queen Califia, described in a romantic novel by the 16th-century Spanish writer Ordonez de Montalvo. The name of the kingdom was, of course, California. Looking at the views to the ocean it is easy to forgive them for imagining they had sailed into a fairy tale. Today the coast is as wild and untamed as it ever was. Gualala, just south of Smugglers Cove (facing page top), has a county park where visitors may enjoy camping and fish in the same river in which Jack London cast for steelhead. A scenic drive northwards from here will pass Elk Cove (left), Elk Creek making its way lazily to the ocean (facing page bottom), and numerous beautiful beaches and bays (below) on the way to Mendocino. Further north stands the picturesque lighthouse at Battery Point (overleaf).

In the case of Mount Shasta (these pages), the tallest mountain of the Cascade Range in northern central California, big is most definitely beautiful. In olden days the Konomihus, Astugewis and Modoc tribes made their homes here. Nowadays people enjoy winter sports, making the most of the area's five glaciers, or just take in the tranquil calm of the alpine setting.

18

Lassen Volcanic National Park (these pages) is an area of wilderness that remains relatively unknown. The vast outdoors is still and silent, the air pure, the great lakes glassy and serene. But it was not always so. In 1915 there was devastation that sent red-hot lava pouring from the mouth of Lassen Peak and twenty-ton boulders crashing down the valleys, along with rivers of warm mud and blankets of ash. The destruction was complete for miles to the east, and even as far as Reno the streets were inches deep in ash.

The 106,000 acres of Lassen Volcanic National Park (these pages) attract curious daytrippers as well as backpackers and adventurers intrigued by this still very active area. The bubbling mud pools and steaming sulfur springs at Bumpass Hell (this page, facing page bottom and overleaf) are an education in themselves. Facing page top: a well-laid-out trail follows the course of a rushing stream.

Lake Tahoe (these pages), on the border with Nevada, is a year-round playground and a joy to visit for anyone with an appreciation of natural beauty. Ringed by the Sierra Nevada to the west, its pine-clad shores are fringed in many places by soft sand beaches (below). Eldorado County beach (below left), Meeks Bay (facing page bottom) and Emerald Bay (remaining pictures) are all popular spots, offering a variety of activities for the visitor. Wherever you are in Tahoe, though, the scenery is second to none.

Sacramento (these pages) began life in the mid-nineteenth century as a gold-rush boom town, and retains much of the atmosphere of by-gone years in its many historic buildings (center left and bottom left). The State Capitol (left and below), completed in 1874, is a glorious example of the Classical Revival style.

The Napa Valley in autumn (overleaf) is a pleasing sight, its neatly combed groves ready for harvest. Ever since 1870 this region has been producing fine wines. Of course there was the slight interruption that came with Prohibition, but today the "Wine that maketh glad the heart of man" is once again big business.

San Francisco (these pages) is arguably the most colorful and cosmopolitan city in the world. It is also, of course, very hilly. The San Franciscans have found various ways to overcome this, and in doing so have produced some unique features, including the "crookedest street in the world" (above). The Golden Gate has long been the symbol of the city, the park (facing page bottom) and the bridge (top right and bottom right) being particularly familiar. Below: Union Square, in the heart of the fine shopping area. Facing page top: Bay Bridge.

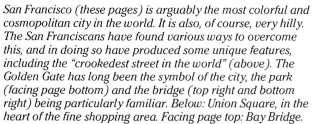

Down by San Francisco Bay there is always something going on, and Fisherman's Wharf (left and above left) is a hive of activity. Inland, cable cars provide a welcome alternative to walking on California Street (above and below). Alcatraz Island (facing page bottom), site of probably the most infamous penitentiary in the world, may be reached by ferry from Pier 41. Guided tours of the island take place daily. For those who prefer to look from a distance, ferries from Pier 39 (bottom left) sail close to the island. Facing page top: the Golden Gate Bridge.

San Francisco's Chinatown (below and center right) is home to the largest population of Chinese outside Asia. It all began with the arrival of two servants aboard the brig Pilgrim *in 1848. By 1854, 25,000 more Chinese immigrants had made their homes in the state they called the "Gold Mountain." The restaurants and shops to be found here are some of the best of their kind. Twilight in San Francisco can bathe the Bay Bridge (right) and Alamo Square (bottom right) in delicate pastel tones.*

These pages: the timeless beauty of Yosemite, surely the best known and best loved of all America's national parks. El Capitan (left, above and overleaf) rises to an elevation of 7,569 feet opposite Bridalveil Falls. However, it is Yosemite Falls (facing page) that really have to be seen to be believed – the upper falls alone tumble over a drop greater than nine times that of Niagara! Half Dome (below), by Mirror Lake, is a dazzling spectacle.

The sequoia tree is the largest of all living things and is a sight to marvel at in the Sequoia National Park (facing page, above, below and top right), established in 1890 to preserve these giants. Both Sequoia and Kings Canyon national parks (right and bottom right) are part of the Sierra Nevada, a dramatic mountain range. General Grant Tree, from which Grant Grove (right) takes its name, is second in size only to General Sherman Tree (facing page). Below: the Four Guardsmen dwarf a van of sightseers.

Just south of Carmel on Highway One lies Point Lobos State Reserve (facing page top and right), six miles of glorious, rugged coast beaten by tempestuous Pacific waves. It is a nature reserve of some distinction, being of particular interest to the ornithologist and, in November, the whale-watcher. The great California gray whales pass close by the coast on their way to the Baja, where they spend the winter. Highway One bends and twists along the coastline, offering many inspiring views of the ocean. Pull-ins are located at vantage points along the way, including one at magnificent Bixby Creek Bridge (facing page bottom). North of Carmel lies Pacific Grove (below), which holds a "Butterfly Parade" in October when thousands of these insects arrive to make their homes there for the winter. Further north still, at Gray Whale Cove (overleaf), excellent bathing is to be had.

Solvang (left) is a Danish Community that lies about thirty miles northwest of Santa Barbara in the Santa Ynez Valley. Its picturesque thatched houses, interesting little shops and old-fashioned windmill make it well worth a visit. Santa Barbara itself is a classic Spanish mission town with a fine waterfront (facing page). Another Franciscan mission, San Carlos Borromeo del Río Carmelo (below), may be found in Carmel. This late-18th-century sandstone church has undergone complete restoration and now offers a fascinating monument to the days before its secularization. It is hard to believe that the hands that built it were those of "unskilled" laborers. Particularly notable features include the cell of Father Junípero Serra, the first library of California, and the Moorish-influenced tower. It was Father Junípero Serra who, along with Gaspar de Portolá, established the first of the state's Spanish presidios on the south shore of Monterey Bay. Monterey was California's number one city until the 1848 gold strike caused San Francisco to take precedence. These days it is renowned for its fine waterfront (overleaf).

Think of California: sand, sun and sea. It's no wonder people return again and again to the beautiful Pacific beaches to watch the sun rise or set, to walk the pier, try for a fish or just to be a part of the landscape knowing they're in one of the loveliest places in the world. Santa Monica (center right) has long been a popular resort for the people of Los Angeles, a haven from the busy city. Further north, Malibu Beach (right) is known world-wide as a place of secluded beauty favored by the rich and famous. Pismo (bottom right) and Manhattan (below) beaches offer evening tranquility.

Los Angeles (these pages) is the biggest city on the west coast, which in California means BIG. It's the home of Disneyland (left bottom and below), Hollywood (above), and Beverley Hills – places dreams are made of. There are state-of-the-art hotels like the Bonaventure (left), grand sporting venues such as the Memorial Coliseum (top left) and busy, all-American streets like Western Avenue (facing page bottom). The city also has its own Chinatown (facing page top). Overleaf: Palm Springs.

"Death Valley" (these pages) is an emotive name for an inspiring place. Whether its forbidding vastness leaves them fearful or elated, this national monument has a profound effect upon each and every one of its visitors. At the northern end of the valley lies Mediterranean-style Scotty's Castle (right), built in the 1920s by Albert Johnson and named for Walter "Death Valley" Scott, who lived there until his death in 1954. Not far away from the castle lies the 800-foot-deep Ubehebe Crater (center right). The strange geological formations at Zabriskie Point (below) and the Devil's Golf Course (bottom right) also merit a visit. Overleaf: Joshua Tree National Monument.

San Diego (these pages, overleaf and following page) has a great deal to offer, from the oldest of the Californian missions (above) to the Moonlight State Beach (bottom right) and quaint La Jolla (below), renowned for its artistic heritage. The Spanish baroque Casa del Prado (right) in Balboa Park and the Victorian Hotel del Coronado (top right and facing page top) together illustrate the diversity of the city's heritage. Overleaf: a night-view across San Diego Bay reveals the downtown district in all its splendor.